This Christmas Coloring Book
Belongs To:

____

____

Date: _______ / ____ / ______

Write and Draw to Express Yourself

Date: ___/___/___

Write and Draw to Express Yourself

Date: ___ / ___ / ___

Date: ______ / ______ / ______

Write and Draw to Express Yourself

Date: _____ / __ / __

Write and Draw to Express Yourself

Date: _____ / ____ / _____

Date: _____/_____/_____

Write and Draw to Express Yourself

Date: ___/___/___

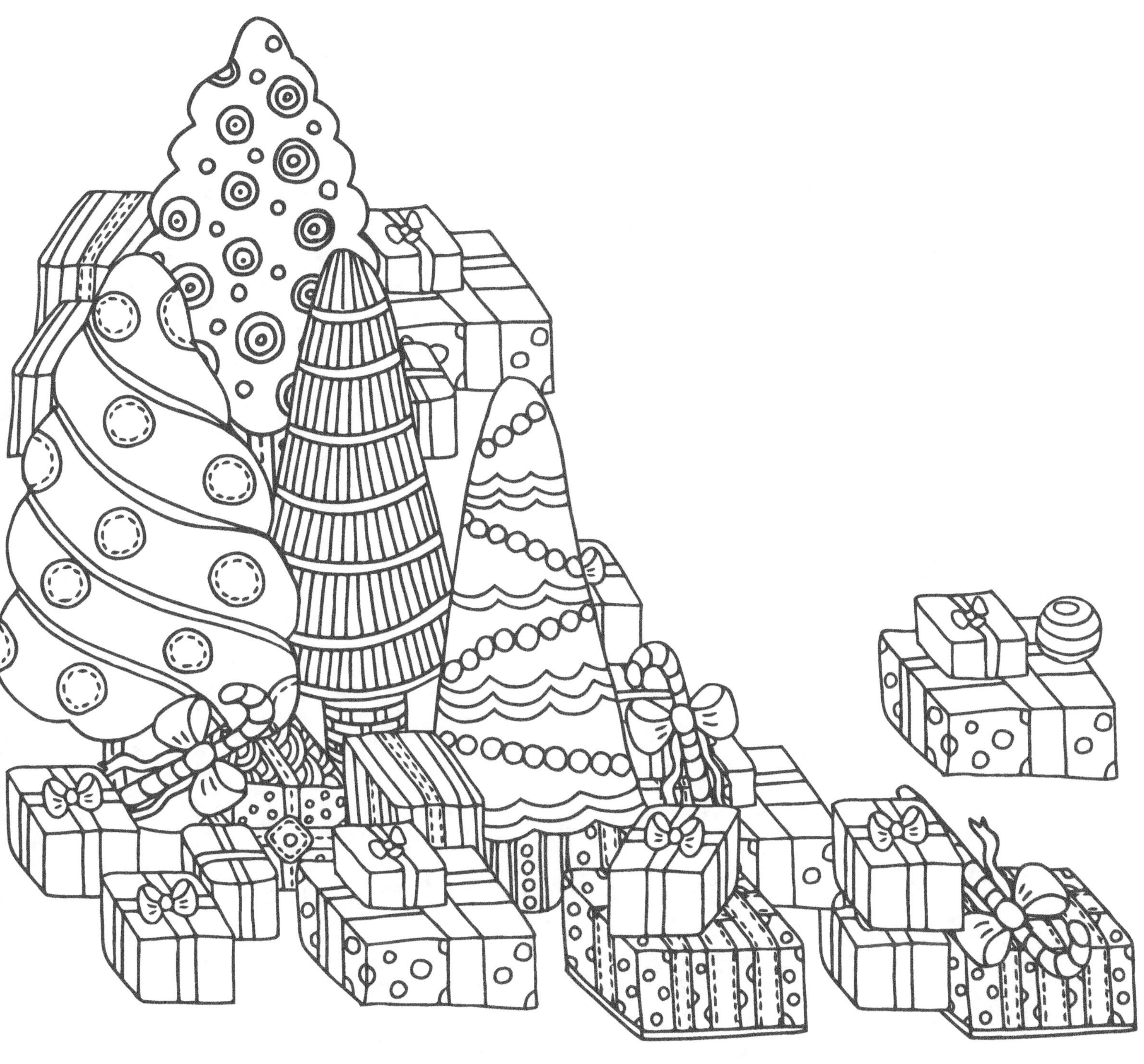

Write and Draw to Express Yourself

Date: ___/___/___

Date: _______ / ___ / _______

Write and Draw to Express Yourself

Date: ___ / ___ / ___

Date: _______/____/____

Write and Draw to Express Yourself

Date:

xmas

Write and Draw to Express Yourself

Date:

Write and Draw to Express Yourself

Date: _______ / _______ / _______

Date: ____ / ____ / ____

Write and Draw to Express Yourself

Date: ___ / ___ / ___

Christmas
Time

Date: ___/___/___

Write and Draw to Express Yourself

Date: _______ / _____ / _____

Write and Draw to Express Yourself

Write and Draw to Express Yourself

Date: _______ / ___ / ___

Write and Draw to Express Yourself

Date: ___ / ___ / ___

Merry Christmas

Date: _______ / ____ / ____

Write and Draw to Express Yourself

Date: ___/___/___

Write and Draw to Express Yourself

Date:

Write and Draw to Express Yourself

Date: ___ / ___ / ___

Date: ___/___/___

Write and Draw to Express Yourself

Date: ___ / ___ / ___

Write and Draw to Express Yourself

Date: _____/_____/_____

Write and Draw to Express Yourself

Date: _____ / ___ / ___

Date: ___/___/___

Write and Draw to Express Yourself

Write and Draw to Express Yourself

Write and Draw to Express Yourself

Date: _____ / ___ / ___

Write and Draw to Express Yourself

The Magic of Christmas

Write and Draw to Express Yourself

Date: ___________ / _____ / __________

Write and Draw to Express Yourself

Date:

Date: _____ / ___ / _____

Write and Draw to Express Yourself

Write and Draw to Express Yourself

Write and Draw to Express Yourself

Date: ___ / ___ / ___

Date: _______ / ___ / _______

Write and Draw to Express Yourself

Date: ___/___/___

Date: ___/___/___

Write and Draw to Express Yourself

Date: ___ / ___ / ___

Write and Draw to Express Yourself

Date: _____ / _____ / _____

Write and Draw to Express Yourself

Write and Draw to Express Yourself

peace
&
joy

Write and Draw to Express Yourself

Date:

Date: ___/___/___

Write and Draw to Express Yourself

Date: ___ / ___ / ___

Date: ___/___/___

Date: ___ / ___ / ___

Write and Draw to Express Yourself

Date: ___/___/___

Write and Draw to Express Yourself

Date: _____ / ___ / ___

Write and Draw to Express Yourself

Date:

Date: ___/___/___

Write and Draw to Express Yourself

Date: ___/___/___